Stop Screwing Around

and

Win

Your Next
Screenplay Contest!

Your Step-by-step Guide to Winning
Hollywood's Biggest Competitions

By
Robert L. McCullough

How to *WIN* Your Next Screenplay Contest

First printing edition 2018

This book is written in Microsoft Word using Courier Screenwriter, the standard font in use throughout the film and television industry.

Also by the author:

Stop Screwing Around and
Write a Screenplay That Sells!

Where Hollywood Hides: Celebrities in Paradise
(co-author Suzanne Herrera-McCullough)

Copyright © 2018 Butterfly Beach Media
All rights reserved.
ISBN: 9781723716447

Butterfly Beach Media
1187 Coast Village Rd. Ste. 512
Santa Barbara, Ca. 93108
www.stop-screwing-around-and-write.com

Table of Contents

Before We Begin..1

Preface 9

Acknowledgements..13

1. Why Enter Any Contest?...17

2. Ask The Tough Questions 25

    Who? 26

    What? 27

    Where? 28

    When? 29

    Why? 31

3. Have a Clear Concept 35

4. Formatting Matters! 41

5. Your Characters Count 47

6. Know Your Structure 51

7. Write a Killer Logline 55

8. Don't Do This Stuff 59

    Over-provide your contact info................. 61

    Include WGA Registration Numbers............ 61

    Write your logline on the cover page... 62

    Put artwork on a fancy cover...................... 62

Include scene numbers 63

Include scene and character breakdowns or set lists 64

Indicate "Credits". 64

Use colored paper 65

Write detailed stage directions 65

Write in a literary style. 66

Over-use technical vocabulary 67

Write dialogue with unnecessary "wrylies". 67

Use redundant/repeated transition slugs 68

Get "creative" with transitions 68

Write what can't be shot 69

9. Don't Write the Wrong Stuff 73

Superhero action 74

Installments of existing franchises 75

Sequels 76

Adaptations of prior works you don't own 77

Animation projects 77

10. Don't Submit Your Script Until It's Ready 81

Afterword 93

Frequently Asked Questions 105

About the Author 111

Before We Begin...

You bought this book because you're a screenwriter and you're ready to see it produced and to collect that nice, fat paycheck.

Oh, and let's not forget your walk down The Red Carpet to accept your Academy Award or Emmy.

Of course, first you've got to write something and by now you've figured out that Hollywood hasn't been sitting around waiting for you and your screenplay to grace the industry with your insanely creative brilliance. You've discovered that the life of a screenwriter hoping to become the next Aaron Sorkin is every bit as challenging as that of an actor hoping to become the next Jennifer Lawrence or Ryan Gosling.

This is not a book for those with delusions of any kind. Nor is it a book for those hoping to learn *how* to write a screenplay (for that, you should read *Stop Screwing Around and Write a Screenplay That Sells!,* available at www.stop-screwing-around-and-write.com/screenwriting and at Amazon.com).

This book is for those who understand the fundamental realities of today's Hollywood film industry and who are ready to generate some "heat" by submitting their scripts to the best screenplay competitions they can find.

Okay, so how can you generate the "heat" that gets you and your screenplay noticed?

Great question. I thought you'd never ask.

Gone are the days of Hollywood agents going home each night after a grueling day of making deals for clients with a stack of unsolicited screenplays by unknown writers in the hope of finding their next star client. Gone are the days of major studio development executives spending their weekends reading "over the transom" submissions. Gone are the days of bankable actors meeting a writer on the tennis court and two days later striding into a studio president's office with a script and declaring "This is my next film!"

Like everything else in the world, the movie business has changed.

Unsolicited material (your screenplay) just doesn't get read. If you send your completed masterpiece to any major studio, you'll hear crickets. Nothing. The vacuum of intergalactic space.

If you send that same script with a self-addressed stamped envelope and a perfectly lovely and engaging cover letter of introduction detailing your lifelong appreciation for the art of film and for dramatic/comedic screen craft, you *might* get your envelope back in the mail with a simple and very brief letter, to wit: "Thank you for your interest in The Awesome Literary Agency. Unfortunately, we do not accept unsolicited submissions. Best of luck with your writing."

That's just not the way it's done any more. Why not?

In 1988 there was a protracted strike by professional screenwriters working under Writers Guild of America contracts. Studios and producers were soon desperate for material. Any pre-existing material (not written during the term of the strike) was suddenly worth something, simply because it was ready to shoot.

Scripts began fetching very impressive prices, with many being sold for millions from both seasoned writers as well as from newbies. Publicity ensued. People who had been writing ad copy or poetry or short stories, or who were toiling in the groves of academia teaching others how to write, immediately began writing screenplays.

By the time the Writers Guild strike was over, the torrent of screenplays piling up in mailboxes and littering desks all over Hollywood became impossible for the studios and agents to deal with.

A filtering system that could separate the wheat from the chaff was needed...and the world of screenwriting contests was born.

Today, there are hundreds of screenplay competitions offering writers a way to have their material judged, rated, ranked, and promoted. It is now the system that provides the reading and analysis formerly conducted by agents and development executives.

The Hollywood film industry loves screenplay competitions simply because they are an effective filtering system wherein only the best scripts rise to the top of the heap. A screenwriter who wins a major screenplay competition suddenly become visible to producers and studios.

Writers who win reputable screenplay competitions demonstrate both talent and marketability. If the film industry worked on a logical basis, these are screenwriters would see their movies produced.

Winning writers know two things: how to write a professional screenplay and *how to win* a major screenplay competition.

In this book, I'm going to share the secrets and fundamentals you need to follow if you're serious about winning a script contest.

You might not like what you read in these pages, but trust me on this: the hype and the bullshit stop right here.

What I'm going to share now is just the simple truth because I want you to stop screwing around and *win* your next screenplay contest.

If that's your goal, this is the book for you.

No single movie or event makes or breaks your career. Everything can be undone, including success.

~ Linda Obst, feature film producer

How to *WIN* Your Next Screenplay Contest

Preface

This book is going to be short and to the point. It doesn't need to be 490 pages long (thank you, Robert McKee for writing a 2-lb doorstop), so it won't be. You just don't have time to keep reading about *how* to do something; you need to stop screwing around and *do* it.

I'll do my best to keep things civil here, but I can't make too many promises in that regard; it's a tough business, this screenwriting stuff, and you need to be ready to hear it like it truly is.

What I *am* going to say is the bottom-line truth, because I personally don't have the patience for the usual hype and nonsense you'll hear at the endless and redundantly self-serving seminars, symposia, lectures, and "networking" sessions that do zilch for your chances of winning a script contest.

Winning your next screenplay competition can (and should) change your life.

I'm going to show you how to make sure that happens.

How to *WIN* Your Next Screenplay Contest

*Failure is a badge of honor;
it means you risked failure.*

~ Charlie Kaufman, screenwriter

How to *WIN* Your Next Screenplay Contest

Acknowledgements

A screenwriter turns his work over to others to judge, to edit, to rewrite, and ultimately to translate into moving images. A prose writer—what I am here in these pages—owns every word, but needs the feedback and help of others to stay on track and to make sure the message is getting across and is of value to the reader.

None of what follows would have been possible without the help and insights of my wife and frequent collaborator, Suzanne Herrera-McCullough.

As a Senior Judge at The Los Angeles International Screenplay Awards with her own TV and film credits, Suzanne's perspectives contributed immensely to all that follows. She's the one who pulled me back from my usual rantings and made sure I kept it all on point.

If you get anything out of this book, it's thanks to her.

How to *WIN* Your Next Screenplay Contest

It's possible for me to make a bad movie out of a good script, but I can't make a good movie from a bad script.

~ George Clooney, actor-producer

How to *WIN* Your Next Screenplay Contest

1. Why Enter Any Contest?

Excellent question.

After all, *you're* the writer. You've seen a lot of movies, maybe even read a handful of scripts written by screenwriters who get paid for their work. And you've got all the latest screenwriting software, and probably have a nice soft-touch keyboard attached to a very slick computer that allows your creative juices to flow.

And after you've opened the floodgates to those creative juices, you hit the Print Key and the next thing you know, you have a screenplay in hand with your name on the cover page.

At least it *looks* like a screenplay and it *feels* like a screenplay.

And now you want to know just how good your script is, so maybe you ask your Uncle George to give your screenplay a thorough read-through. Of course, the fact that Uncle George is an amazing Certified Public Accountant, or a lawyer, or a nuclear medicine oncologist means he's a pretty smart guy who should know a good script from a dud.

But he doesn't. He might even like movies and have a long list of favorites. But he doesn't know *why* he likes them, or what makes them interesting enough for him to even remember.

So when Uncle George reads your script, you're going to get a rave review, a pat on the back, and all kinds of encouragement because...well, he's your Uncle George.

But Uncle George doesn't read screenplays as a part of his daily professional life, he's never written one, never sold one, and never seen his own work go into production with a multi-million-dollar budget behind it.

That's why I beg you: don't give your script to Uncle George. He's a busy guy, and all you're going to hear in response—if he ever actually gets around to reading your screenplay—is what a wonderful writer you are.

Uncle George's opinion, frankly, is completely meaningless and a colossal waste of your time.

That's just one reason why you need to submit your scripts to as many reputable screenplay competitions as you can afford.

Of course, entering your screenplay for professional review, appraisal, and competition among your writing peers is not without cost. Submission fees can range anywhere from a few dollars to a few hundred dollars, with most in the range of $50-$85. Those fees generally cover the cost of data management, administration, prize money, and varying levels of reader analysis.

In today's world, unless you have professional representation at an industry literary agency, breaking into the world of professional screenwriting is a complicated process involving a very steep uphill climb.

The most viable route up that steep hill is to place well in one or more of the reputable competitions accepting open submissions.

Yes, entry fees into these competitions can add up; consider them an investment in your career. And the return on that investment can be significant.

By doing well in a contest, you can often receive free publicity and promotion, enjoy mentorship under industry notables, and make valuable connections.

And even if you don't win the brass ring, the better competitions feature judges who are all working film and television professionals. These are the people you *want* to read your material, and you simply can't predict what might happen if your script gets into the right judge's hands.

The other advantage of entering the right competition is that you can request a professional, written evaluation of your script *before* it even goes into the contest.

Those analytical appraisals, written after a thorough, word-by-word reading in the hands of someone highly experienced in assessing the writing craftsmanship and realistic market potential of your script, is often worth more than any possible prize money.

How to *WIN* Your Next Screenplay Contest

*If it sounds like writing,
I rewrite it.*

~ Elmore Leonard, screenwriter

How to *WIN* Your Next Screenplay Contest

2. Ask The Tough Questions

The world of journalism has something for everyone who has screenwriting ambitions. Seems logical, since both disciplines involve, to one degree or another, a search for the truth.

Before we dive into the nitty-gritting of winning that next screenplay contest, you need to ask yourself the five questions every journalist must answer when reporting a story:

> Who?
> What?
> Where?
> When?
> Why?

Okay, let's start at the beginning…

Who?

Who are you as a writer?

Are you the writer who will persist until someone finally gives you either meaningful recognition (a *job* as a writer is my definition of "meaningful") or at least detailed feedback so you can start the real work of rewriting?

If that's who you are, you're a unique writer. You've cleared that hurdle. You may even have what it takes to truly find success as a screenwriter.

What?

Okay, you're a screenwriter. But *what* are you going to write about?

If you have some point of view, or a statement about a certain set of interpersonal relationships, or a new insight into an historical event or epoch, or a character in your heart that speaks to the burning emotions within you, then you have a handle on your *what*.

Don't let go of that handle, because it will pull you through the hard work, frustration, and challenges that lie in wait for you far beyond "Fade In".

Where?

No, this isn't about the location of that story you're determined to tell or where your desk is located. The question is *where are you as a writer?*

You must be realistic about your chances of selling your work, of seeing it produced, and of ever being paid for a second screenplay.

Where you are is where everybody is at this stage of the game. At the bottom. On the outside looking in, filled with passion and big dreams.

That's okay. You *can* sell your script. All you have to do is write it, get it noticed, and be ready to write another. As a screenwriter, even after you've made a sale and seen your work produced, *where* you are never changes: writing the next one.

When?

This is another question only you can answer for yourself, The Screenwriter With Big Ideas.

And whatever the answer may be, it's the only one that is completely within your control.

Have you always dreamed of "working in the movies" but have never really figured out how to get there … until you heard that "having a script" is the fastest way inside those studio gates (which happens to be true)?

As soon as you heard that, what did you do? Did you buy some books about screenwriting and discover that they're nearly always written by people who have very limited personal experience as a professional screenwriter?

Did you spend weeks and months reading those books before sitting down to write…because you wanted to "get it right"?

Here's a newsflash: that's called pro-cras-tin-ation and it's your worst enemy. The point is a simple one: real screenwriting requires *writing* and writing (sigh) is hard work.

Once you've spent all the time, energy, and money it takes to *avoid* the hard work of writing, the question remains: when?

When are you going to set aside all the easy excuses? When are you going to stop checking your email, answering the phone, walking the dog, washing the car, reading books, taking classes, going to the gym, and sit down and finally sit down and do the hard work?

If you're serious about screenwriting, today is your *when*.

Why?

Do you want to write a screenplay because...

- It's the best way to break into showbiz?
- You've heard the money is good?
- You simply love writing?
- Movies are in your blood?
- You can do better than the stuff that's out there now?

If any of those are your reasons for writing your screenplay, you'll be much happier if you do something else with your time.

Those are simply not tenable motivations to see you travel the road before you.

But if the absolute rock-bottom line is that you're going to do this no matter what the odds are, no matter what warnings I give you, no matter how much your family and friends advise against it, no matter what other wonderful options in life you may have...then you have your *why*: it's something you *must do* to feel fulfilled, that life is worth living.

If that's truly your *why*, then let me welcome you to the world I live in: the world of the professional screenwriter.

*One of the most difficult things for
a writer in this business to accept
is the uncertain fate
of one's work.*

~ Michael Crichton, screenwriter

3. Have a Clear Concept

Whatever you do, don't submit a screenplay to any competition that lacks a truly tangible, clear-cut, compelling premise and concept.

This is the one element of your script that either catapults it above all others in the competition you're entering ... or that makes it sink like a rock in the deep waters of seen-it-all-before.

But what makes a winning "concept" and what makes it compelling enough for you to invest your hard work into turning it into a contest-winning screenplay?

Your concept is what the movie is *about*. It needs to be so clear that you can express it in a sentence or two. That sentence or two (never more then three) becomes your *logline*, and it needs to be so carefully written and constructed that it reads fluently and with great economy.

Your concept must be so clear that it leaps out of the logline at first glance (that's how much time many competition readers will give you) and *forces* the reader to open the script to find out if you can really deliver what you've promised.

At their core, concepts are the simple, easily-articulated building blocks of thoughts and beliefs.

A meaningful concept is the principle, the driving force behind something that the screenwriter needs to coalesce and present to the reader in the most clear-cut and dramatic way possible as *the idea behind the story*.

Your concept should be easily expressed, and immediately understood by your reader. It's the "general idea" of your movie.

Something we frequently see in screenplay competitions is a great concept…with no real story.

Just because you have an amazing concept, until you can define the elements of a compelling premise, you don't really have a story at all.

Screenplay contest readers and judges will fall all over themselves if you have a concept supporting a premise that makes them sit up and take notice, and if you have articulated it clearly.

Now all you have to do is write the script and not make any of the common mistakes that will eliminate it from the winners' circle of any reputable competition.

How to *WIN* Your Next Screenplay Contest

Hollywood is the only town where you cannot fail. You can only quit trying.

~ Dennis Foley, screenwriter

4. Formatting Matters!

Get your hands on a professionally-written screenplay well before you submit your killer script to any screenplay competition.

We live in a great "information age" because—unlike the pre-computer age when you either had to be working on a studio lot or know someone in the industry just to get your hands on a script—today there are plenty of online resources available where you can source any number of screenplays to your favorite movies (start with http://www.awesomefilm.com/).

Once you open the cover, you can't help but notice how a professionally written screenplay looks: page numbers in upper right of every page after the first one. (Page numbering starts with 2 on the second page.) Wide margins all the way around. Dialogue indented and centered. Dialogue headers in FULL CAPS.

When you're submitting to a screenplay competition, you're not giving your script to a bunch of studio technicians who are going to begin to immediately budget their departmental costs for production.

Your script is going to be read by (hopefully) highly-skilled, seasoned Hollywood readers who understand today's marketplace and who have an intimate understanding of screenwriting excellence.

Your script is a "spec" script. You have great hopes for it, but you've haven't been paid to write it, and it hasn't yet been produced. So you have all the freedom in the world to write your script as you see fit, but there are a number of very strict rules about how it needs to be formatted.

Before you submit your screenplay to any contest, make sure you have a solid grasp of formatting standards…and follow them.

When you write with the proper, industry-standard formatting style expected by competition judges, your scripts will look like the work of a professional.

Never submit your original work in any software formatting or editing program (Word, Final Draft, Movie Magic, etc.).

Submit your finished work to screenplay competitions *only* as a PDF file.

You're submitting a *reading script*, not a shooting script. Don't get creative, don't use "interesting" fonts or make any part of the reading process challenging for the readers or judges. Be typical in this respect and make your script easy to read.

Follow industry formatting standards, and you'll be ahead of the competition from FADE IN.

If you need specifics on how to accomplish this, just check out the first book in this series, *Stop Screwing Around and Write Your Screenplay*, where I lay all of that out in easy-to-follow detail.

How to *WIN* Your Next Screenplay Contest

*When I feel like being a director,
I write a novel.*

~ John Irving, author-screenwriter

5. Your Characters Count

I see a lot of screenplays that tell an amazing story. They take place in highly unusual settings with amazing action sequences swirling around compelling, dramatic issues. Many even have clever, brilliant dialogue that either makes you cry or has you laughing out loud.

In spite of all that, they're all a complete bore to read. Because they don't have characters the reader can care about, they'll never get produced, nor will they ever win any credible screenplay competition.

This book isn't designed to teach you how to write great characters (that's all in the book *Stop Screwing Around and Write Your Screenplay*), but keep this in mind when you're submitting to a contest:

Make sure your reader knows very quickly—within the first ten pages—who, what, and why.

WHO is the protagonist? WHAT is his/her goal?

WHY does he/she need to accomplish the goal?

Be sure you can answer those questions *before* you submit to any competition.

You can never know enough about your characters.

~ W. Somerset Maugham, author

How to *WIN* Your Next Screenplay Contest

6. Know Your Structure

By the point at which you're reading this book about winning a screenplay competition, you're obviously aware of the issue of story structure.

So I'm not going to bore you with a treatise on the importance of it here. You know that without a *beginning, middle,* and *end*, your screenplay is going to have a difficult time with competition readers and judges.

Why is that?

Because every screenplay is something like a house of cards; one misplaced element, one slip, and the whole thing falls in on itself.

A screenplay is a collection of interdependent elements; each one affects the other. Each of those elements comes to life in a series of causes and effects and none can come to life without the other.

To have the best possible shot at winning your next screenplay competition, check your structure to make sure that:

- Your script grabs the reader's attention at the very beginning. Those first ten pages are the *key* to the reader moving on.
- You're keeping the reader off-balance. If the reader can guess where it's all going at any point in the story, you have a structural problem.

Building the proper dramatic structure (this applies to comedies too) takes careful planning and a complete understanding of your characters.

Structuring your story is a critical first step. Give it the attention it requires and you'll give yourself the best chance of success in any competition.

*"Once you crack the script,
everything else follows."*

~ Ridley Scott

7. Write a Killer Logline

With the tsunami of scripts showing up in screenplay competitions today, a good logline has never been more important.

The simple fact is that without a good logline, your script will certainly never make it to the "selected" or semi-final categories of a truly competitive contest.

You're probably wondering "how is that possible?"

As a writer, you need to understand just how many scripts cross a reader's desk and are forwarded to senior judging panels on a weekly basis.

The numbers can be daunting: estimates as high as 10,000 scripts per *day* are submitted to the handful of quality competitions throughout the country (and that's not counting the scripts hapless hopefuls send to the insanely crappy—and marginally fraudulent—contests created by clowns who have never been inside the gates of any studio and who are building "contest" websites on a laptop in their parents' basement).

Do the math: 10,000 scripts going to the better, established competitions featuring qualified readers and *bona* fide industry professionals. And then another 10,000 scripts going nowhere at "contests" run by scamsters and amateurs. That's a lot of reading, which means that some contest readers (many of whom have zero industry background and work as unpaid interns, mind you) only have time to review your logline.

Considering those numbers, your logline had better be pretty damned good.

Writing a great logline requires a bit of art and science. There's a lot to know about it if you want to do it correctly. Far too much to deal with here. I cover all the details about writing a winning logline in *Stop Screwing Around and Write Your Screenplay*.

You want your script to have the best chance of getting a "full read" in whatever competition you enter.
To give yourself that chance, keep your logline simple and to the point, and *make us want to know more*.

A professional writer is an amateur who didn't quit.

~ Richard Bach

8. Don't Do This Stuff

Hollywood—just like any number of work environments where there are big rewards for excellent performance—is a world of perceptions.

When you walk down the sidewalks of any American city and you see someone well-dressed of a professional bearing, you immediately get a feeling about them. And the guy lying in the gutter sucking on a bottle of rotgut whiskey while screaming at the sun gives you another feeling.

Your script is no different.

Screenplay contest readers and judges get an immediate impression about you and about your material the moment they pick up your script or open it up on their laptop screen.

If your script reflects any of the following mistakes, you'll be immediately consigned to the ranks of an amateur in the minds of those judging your script.

In all likelihood, of course, you *are* an amateur. You've never sold anything, never had anything produced, and probably aren't even close to getting an agent to rep your stuff.

But that's okay! We're all amateurs at one point in our careers. Everyone has to begin somewhere. You're not expected to be perfect or to present a screenplay that is so flawless that every major studio in town begins throwing money at you.

That kind of thing happens…but on a level of frequency comparable to asteroids striking The White House (Wait! There's a movie idea!).

What you want, however, is for your material to be judged on its merits. You don't want your script tossed aside because of something superficial that marks you as a rank amateur who hasn't even taken the time to study the craft to the point where you easily avoid glaring mistakes.

So here's an ugly little secret: When an experienced writing-producing-directing-development professional opens your script, it takes 45-60 seconds to tell whether or not you have a freaking *clue* about what you're doing…and whether they should bother reading it at all.

How do you keep a reader's attention beyond that 60-second mark? It's really just a matter of not violating a small handful of unspoken rules when preparing your script to send out.

Ignore these rules and you'll be immediately spotted as an amateur who doesn't know what's expected in a screenplay. So *don't do these things:*

Over-provide your contact info. Be sure your name is on the title page, centered. Be sure your phone and email address are in the lower right corner of the title page. You want people to be able to find you, don't you? A script with no name or contact info on the cover is immediately rejected. You may have written the next *Hell or High Water* (Taylor Sheridan, 2017), but it won't matter because nobody is going to read it. Conversely, don't overdo it. Just one phone number, please, not your landline, your mobile number, your work phone, your parents' number, or an "emergency phone." Email address and phone number. That's it.

Include WGA Registration Numbers. Your name is on the cover. We know who wrote the script and where we can contact you when we're ready to make a deal and write you a check. But appearing like a paranoid more concerned about being ripped off by some unscrupulous mustache-twirling producer than about telling a great story and building a solid collaborative filmmaking relationship is a complete turn-off. Nobody cares if you register with the WGA, or if you jump through the hoops to register your work with the U.S. Copyright Office. A WGA Registration number might impress *you*, but it tell the reader you don't trust him/her and you're ready to sue anyone who doesn't make your movie. Don't do it. It's the mark of a loser. Yes, you can register your script, copyright it, trademark it…whatever. Just don't put that stuff on the cover.

Write your logline on the cover page. Eegads. Tell the reader what he/she is about to read, and they won't read any further. Your logline—while very important as discussed elsewhere here—is your tool for pitching and for keeping you focused during the writing process. Don't even put your logline on the first inside page. It will simply stop the reader from turning that page because they "already know what it's all about." And nobody ever won a screenplay competition by *not* getting their script read!

Put artwork on a fancy cover. You may think it would be cool to deliver your script with an embossed leather cover. Or in that day-glo binder that caught your eye at Office Max. Don't do it. Professionals simply use a standard piece of paper for their script cover. This is the moment to blend in with the crowd. Let your *writing* be what makes your script rise to the top, not some lame cover art or flashy colors. Three-hole paper held together by simple brass brads. No staples, no tricky fasteners. This is where simplicity is the key to genius.

Include scene numbers. Easily spotted on the first page, and a sure sign of an amateur. Today's screenwriting software makes it easy to include them, but just because you *can* doesn't mean you *should*. Do NOT include scene numbers on any page of your script. Scene numbers are critically important once your script goes into production, but you're not going into production at this point; you're trying to win a screenplay contest so that your script will have a shot at someday winding up in the hands of the right people. Until your spec script gets financing, casting, a director, and a production team, it has *no business* using scene numbers. Sure, they look cool, but they're *meaningless and distracting* in a spec script. Professional readers, producers, and studio executives are insulted by scene numbers on a script that doesn't have a greenlight. Don't use them. Just number the pages in the upper right corner beginning on page 2.

Include scene and character breakdowns or set lists. Cast list. Location list. Prop list. Day/night breakdowns. *None* of that has anything to do with getting your story into the head of the individual reading the script. Not only is it a lot of work to build those lists, but *any* list either at the beginning of your script or in some sort of "appendix" will simply distract the reader's attention, make your script more difficult to read, and mark you as an overreaching amateur. Remember, your script must *read* well before anyone will ever respond to it. Let the producers, the casting directors, and the prop department make the lists. You're the *writer*. Your job is to tell a compelling story that they simply can't put down until FADE OUT. Nothing more.

Indicate "Credits". Your screenplay is designed (if you're smart about winning) to be *read*. Yes, you need to write visually and cinematically, but don't indicate in the opening pages where the onscreen titles and credits should appear. That will immediately jerk the reader out of the story at a time when you need to really get the ball rolling and draw the reader into your characters and the action at hand. Not only will inserting scene slugs where you think the credits should go take up valuable page length, but you're not ever going to be the one to decide such things. That's what producers and directors do. The same thing goes for the "credit roll" at the end of your movie. We don't need to know where it starts or what's on it. That's someone else's job…after your movie has been made.

Use colored paper. Your script should be on *white paper only*. Scripts with varying page colors are already under contract and paid for. Those colors are used by studios and producers to indicate the order of any rewrites made after the original "first draft." Yes, you may have made dozens upon dozens of changes to your script since you first wrote it. That's what writers do: they rewrite. But the script you submit to your next competition should not reflect that series of rewrites. White paper only.

Write detailed stage directions. Stage directions (the stuff that sits right below the all-caps "scene slug" need to be simple, straightforward, and easy to read at a glance. Long paragraphs of single-spaced ink are a complete turn-off. Who wants to open a script that looks like homework in an AP History class? Don't fall into the trap of writing instructions for actors telling them how they're supposed to "look" or "feel" in a scene, or how you want the director to place the camera or block the movements of characters. Of course, you can indicate action, but *leave something to the imagination*. "The car plunges over the cliff" is sufficient. How the wheels are spinning in relation to Earth's rotation or how the 3mm-sized pea gravel is scattering and in what direction it's flying means nothing. The important thing is that *the car plunges over the cliff*. And if you really want to guarantee that no director will want to work with your material, be sure to include camera directions like PAN LEFT or DOLLY IN or RACK FOCUS.

Write in a literary style. You may have been an English Major or have a particular affinity for iambic pentameter, but writing compound-complex sentences or using arcane language is a serious impediment to ranking well in your screenplay competitions. An overly-literary style almost always slows the reader's progress as he/she looks for the basic information and visual clues that make your words on the page feel like a movie. Distract the reader with high falutin' vocabulary, and you'll lose him. Save the similes and metaphors for your next esoteric thesis on the works of Samuel Pepys or your analysis of Shakespeare's syntax. In the world of screenplay competitions and movies that actually get *made*, putting that stuff into your script just doesn't work.

Over-use technical vocabulary. Like the "prose and poetry" note above, the use of gratuitous technical terminology will bring the reader to a dead halt. Describing the getaway car as a "5.7L Hemi 90-degree pushrod V-8 with active air intake and variable camshaft timing" is not nearly as effective as describing it simply as "faster than hell." Your ability to impress the reader with the depth of your research into internal combustion systems will only work against you unless it is absolutely vital to your characters and to the action around them. Do yourself (and your reader) a favor: just write the story and leave the rest of it to the prop department.

Write dialogue with unnecessary "wrylies". Using parentheticals in dialogue blocks can be a legitimate method of indicating something that may not be inherent in the words to be spoken (of course, the need for them at all might indicate a need for better dialogue!). Referred to as "wrylies" because writers often indicate (wryly) for the actor to understand the tone to be taken with a specific line, this technique generally leads to their overuse and a glorious display of unnecessary adverbs (gently…harshly…wryly) that does nothing more than piss off the director and irritate a good actor. Like overwrought stage directions, wrylies are the mark of a writer trying to direct the movie instead of just telling the best possible story. If you find more than four in your script, kill 'em.

Use redundant/repeated transition slugs. "Cut To" feels really cool to type into your script, I know. But it doesn't mean anything and it takes up valuable space on the page. The reader *knows* that when the script moves from one scene heading to another that a cut is required. That's how films are made. In cuts. One scene stops and another one begins. In between the two, there is a "cut" in the action. Adding "Cut To" between scenes will quickly have your readers slapping themselves on the forehead with "Duh!".

Get "creative" with transitions. Maybe you went to film school and learned the difference between "iris" and "jump cut". Good for you. Now please try to forget all that stuff. It has very little, if anything, to do with writing a script that has a good shot at winning a reputable screenplay competition. When you insert transitions like "Match Cut To" or "Dissolve To" or "Flash Cut", you're going to be perceived as a writer who is trying to direct the script from the comfort of his chair. Should your script ever wind up in the hands of an actual director, it might very well be thrown against the wall in a flurry of shouted vulgarities. (Directors can be touchy that way.) If such transitions are absolutely essential—when writing a flashback scene, for example—us them with caution and on a limited basis.

Write what can't be shot. I'm not talking about the explosion on the damn that lets loose floodwaters that wipe out the town below. That's easily produced with today's computer technology. But when you write that a character "has the courage of a lion earned over his years as a member of the Foreign Legion on duty in the Sinai," the audience will never know that because they're watching your *movie,* not reading your pages. And when you put your reader through the exercise of reading elements that will never make it to the finished film, you're not only wasting valuable space on your pages, you're wasting the reader's time. Avoid writing such fluff by indicating (in this case) his courage through his actions, reactions, and the words of his dialogue. If it can't be shot or translated in words and images on the screen, it doesn't belong in your script.

Avoiding these mistakes is no guarantee that you'll make it to the Finalist or Winner stages of any competition, but make any of these mistakes and I'll guarantee you *won't* become a Finalist or a Winner.

Clutter your blueprint with details better left to others, and your script will look like the cluttered, over-written work of an amateur.

Eliminate these unnecessary elements and your screenplay will appear professional. You'll immediately engage the reader because your screenplay will have genuine promise as a viable script ready for production.

Yes, your script is a blueprint for a brilliant film or television episode. But you're the architect, not the finish carpenter.

*That's one of the nice things about writing,
or any art; if the thing's real,
it just lives.*

~ Woody Allen, writer-director

9. Don't Write the Wrong Stuff

You can write any kind of script you want, okay? It's a free country, The First Amendment, etc. And you can submit a script based upon the subject matter of your choice. The same is true with the genre you choose.

It's all up to you.

But you're reading this book because you want to *win* a screenplay competition and generate some heat for your script and for yourself as a professional-grade writer.

To do that, the script you submit to the contest(s) of your choice must have some reasonable chance of earning the notice of the readers and judges appraising it.

While the marketplace is generally accepting of a very wide range of concepts, stories, characters, and genres, you'll do yourself a favor by not submitting screenplays that fall into any one of the following categories:

Superhero action. There's no doubt that this is one of the most popular genres of the early 21st Century. Given that, everyone and his/her brother/sister (and often his/her mother) is hunched over a keyboard trying to come up with the next *Spiderman* or *Avengers*.

Wouldn't it be wonderful to create the next major superhero franchise that breaks box office records in every country on the planet?

That's just not going to happen, folks. The budgets of superhero movies hover around the $100,000,000 mark. That's a lot of zeros and a lot of money, the kind that only major studio conglomerates can invest (another word for "risk").

Because those studios are managed at the major corporate level and ultimately answer to boards of directors and shareholders, they make their investments based upon proven metrics. The screenplay is frequently the least important element of such productions, because the investment is made pursuant to a proven history of audience interest.

That's why sequels, remakes, and films based upon best-selling books, comic books, and toys are the focus of major studio investment today. These properties are "pre-sold" and can be counted on to generate audience interest at the box office.

Your great idea for an action hero may be better than anything we've ever seen. But it's doubtful we'll ever see it, so submitting such material to a recognized screenplay competition will be promptly identified as the work of a hopeful but unrealistic amateur. So write something else and submit that to give yourself the best chance of winning any screenplay competition.

Installments of existing franchises. Like pre-sold pop culture properties of proven value, studios love proven, profitable franchises because they already have a loyal audience. The *Mission: Impossible* franchise—now at six record-breaking episodes starring Tom Cruise—was based upon the existing, highly successful television franchise.

Studios simply aren't going to be interested in *your* next installment of *Mission: Impossible*, so don't write it and don't submit it to any competition. The readers and judges will look askance at your foolish chutzpah and grade your script accordingly.

You'll be better off writing a great script that has the potential of becoming a franchise, and when your movie gets made and breaks box office records, *then* you can start pumping out the rest of the series.

Sequels. Maybe you've identified a movie that would make a great franchise, so you write the screenplay for the second installment in what you foresee as a long-running series of memorable installments.

Here's why that's a bad idea: if a movie has franchise potential, the producers of that film most assuredly have a script in development for the second film. If they don't, the studio will likely bring the writer back or find an established pro to crank one out just as soon as the first film starts looking good at the box office.

If you should happen to write the greatest sequel of all time, you're not even going to get it read by the studio simply because you're an unknown and they hate hearing from lawyers representing unknowns who think they've been ripped off. Don't write a sequel to any film. Be original and write your *own* amazing characters and premises.

Adaptations of prior works you don't own. Yes, studios and producers love screenplays based upon best-selling books, short stories, or long magazine pieces. But unless you personally option or buy the rights to that material, writing a screenplay from it in the hopes the studio will get the rights for you because your script is so damned good is a fool's game. Don't use material you don't control or you're wasting your time and talent.

Animation projects. Animated films are notoriously expensive to produce. Given that, the major animation studios develop their projects in-house with creative teams involving experienced writers, story board artists, producers, designers, computer graphics engineers, directors, and voice actors. These films generally take years to conceive and create. The studios don't hand these writing assignments out to new screenwriters, and they don't even consider looking at spec work from newcomers.

Writing an animation feature and submitting it to competitions will get your screenplay a nice warm spot at the bottom of the pile, simply because one of the major criteria for a winning script in any competition is *marketability*.

So if you hope to win a screenplay competition that's what *not* to write and submit.

But what *should* you write and submit?

Look at the marketplace. What movies are in the theaters? Which ones are getting good reviews, selling tickets, earning high scores on Rotten Tomatoes?

They won't all be the same. There will be crime movies, action thrillers, suspense-horror films, romantic comedies, family movies. Some will be dismal flops while others will be surprise breakout hits.

I encourage you to pour your blood, sweat, and tears into the one story *you* believe has a chance in the current marketplace. Then submit *that script* to your next screenplay competition.

A great script is absolutely essential, perhaps THE essential thing for a movie to succeed.

~ Sydney Pollack, director

How to *WIN* Your Next Screenplay Contest

10. Don't Submit Your Script Until It's Ready

Okay. You've written your script. You've made sure your characters have clear objectives and are speaking great, scene-progressing dialogue. You're confident—because you've been doing your homework and you've studied the current marketplace—that you now have a clean, highly marketable concept presented in completely professional, industry standard formatting. You've proofread your script multiple times, edited it ruthlessly, and you know you've written FADE OUT at exactly the right place.

At this point, you're going to be pretty darned happy with yourself.

If you're like every other screenwriter out there in the world, you're going to be itching to get it into the hands of a serious director, producer, actor, or studio development executive who can help you move your script onto the fast track to getting it produced.

At the very least, you *know* your script is ready to be entered into one of the more reputable screenplay competitions where industry professional readers are standing by, ready to jump up from their desks, rush into the next room where Senior Judges are waiting for something wonderful to come their way and shout "This is it! We have a winner!"

But wait.

Please.

Don't do it.

Don't click on that *Submit Now* button just yet.

Instead, take a deep breath and set your script aside. Maybe shuffle over to the fridge for a cold one (you've earned it!).

Now…go back to your desk.

Look at the script sitting there. That's your name on the cover. That means something.

You've completed one of the most difficult challenges ever faced by any writer. You've actually *finished* something.

But now…

Let your script sit on your desk for a week.

Go play golf, shop for your next car, head to the gym, or start another script. Anything to distract you, to get your mind off the script you *think* you've just finished.

Then—a week later—open your screenplay and ask a few questions:

- Do you have a unique take on a compelling concept?
- Is your story premise clear by Page 10?
- Do your characters have goals they'll fight for?
- Have you written dialogue that will attract an A-list actor?
- Have you been careful to write your script with standard industry formatting?
- Is your story structured with an identifiable beginning-middle-end?

- Have you written clearly, succinctly, and with an economy of language?
- Have you weeded out any and all clichés?
- Is your script an easy, page-turning read?
- Do you have a stunning logline written down for an eventual pitch?
- Have you proofread your script at least three times?
- Have you had professionals give you a written analysis of your script?

If you can answer those questions in the affirmative, you're now ready to enter and WIN your next screenplay contest.

How can I say that with such confidence?

It's simple: 99% of screenplays submitted to leading competitions fail in one or more critical areas. The majority of writers are simply too anxious to get their material out there without taking the time to make sure their screenplays are truly at the professional level.

It's the 1%--the Finalists and Winners—who understand the rules of the road and who have had their screenplays reviewed and analyzed by working professionals *before* spending good money on entry fees.

So the last question on that list leads to the one at the back of every writer's mind: *do I really need professional script "analysis"?*

Look, I get it. You've put your heart and soul into your script...every page of it. Everybody you've shown it to thinks it's great. All your friends, family members, co-workers...even the ones who didn't actually read it...they all tell you that you've got a sure winner on your hands.

But maybe there's something in the back of your mind...that little voice that won't stop asking about that piece of action, or a clue, or some character motivation that still doesn't quite ring true.

And the only answer you have for that little voice is that you're exhausted or you just don't know how to fix the damned thing, and you really don't want to spend good money just to have some stranger—professional or not—give you yet *another* opinion of your screenplay.

If you've read this far, I hope you've come to trust that everything I'm telling you is true.

So trust me on this: This is precisely where professional script analysis comes into play.

There are established, working Hollywood professionals who are constantly on the hunt for good material. These same pros can spot the flaws and suggest the fixes in your material quickly.

How can they do that when you—the one who has read all the screenwriting books, taken the classes, and had the discipline to sit down and actually *write* the damned thing—can't?

The reason is pretty simple, but it's not something that new writers always enjoy hearing.

It's just that these professionals providing high-level analysis of screenplays have spent their entire careers reading thousands of scripts over the years, produced hundreds of films and TV shows...and have helped writers correct every single script flaw encountered along the way, well before those scripts ever went into production.

What I'm talking about here isn't mere "coverage" that painfully summarizes your screenplay for you. That's easily available through any one of a thousand so-called "script services" you can find online.

Frankly, those people drive me nuts because 99% of them have never written or sold *anything* to anyone. Not a TV pilot, not a feature film screenplay, not a short film, not a documentary, not a treatment, not a logline, not a five-line poem to their local "arts & leisure" throwaway weekly newspaper.

Sorry if I sound irritated, but I'm completely fed up with these scam artists ripping off hard working writers. Send your script to these clowns and you'll get back a page or two of "coverage" which is almost always poorly written and only gives you a summary of your plotline and very little else.

Seriously? Why would you pay for that when you already know exactly what your script is all about?

When you invest in yourself and your work by submitting your screenplay to a team who really knows what they're talking about, and the analysis you get from them points to elements that aren't quite up to professional level, do yourself a favor: don't send it in to any competition just yet.

Frequently, impatient writers will receive analysis of their screenplay that calls for additional rewrites and they ignore the suggestion.

They just *know* their stuff is great and suspect that the reviewers and analysts who have given them professional feedback are "just jealous" or are "trying to rip me off," and they go ahead and start sending their script out to agents, managers, producers, and studio development executives.

Should their script wind up on the desk of a reader at a studio or agency, here's what will happen: If they get any response at all (not likely, because most unsolicited scripts are returned unopened and unread; they simply don't want to deal with amateurs), they'll get a polite but terse email note to the effect that their script "isn't what we're currently looking for." This is simply a polite yet thinly-veiled way of saying that they should have saved a couple of trees rather than fill pages up with their hopeless blather.

If you're lucky enough to get some actual "coverage" from a bona fide agent or development executive, it usually takes the form of a written report, including certain data points that don't even talk about the quality of your writing:

- IDENTIFICATION: Title, Author, Type of Material, Locale, Genre

- LOGLINE: A one sentence summary
- COMMENT SUMMARY: A paragraph summary of the analysis
- BUDGET: The reader's estimated production budget

Then…and here's where the rubber meets the road: There are only two straightforward "grades" given by professional readers after a meaningful appraisal of your script. Producers and studio development executives often will read only that one-word grade when considering your material:

- Recommend.
- Not Recommended.

Fairly self-explanatory, huh? One or the other. Black or white. Up or down.

That's it. All your hard work summed up in one or two words. Your dreams either come true or you get to enjoy the experience commonly called "Hollywood Heartbreak".

If I could reach out from these pages and grab you by the shoulders and look you straight in the eye like a Dutch uncle, I would.

And here's what I would say: *You can avoid that heartbreak by getting professional analysis that includes a close examination of specific issues, including: Format, Structure, Plot, Character, Dialogue, Premise, Pacing, Tone, and (most important of all) Marketability.*

With genuine Professional Analysis, you'll always get multiple pages of carefully structured feedback, analysis, writing critique, and pointers to help you bring your script up to professional standards. Professional Analysis is performed after a careful, time-consuming reading and evaluation of your work. You need the truth about your script's elements, and you deserve proper guidance that enables you to bring the material up to the professional, competitive level.

Often, at the premier level of analysis, the service will include a full hour or more of one-on-one phone or Skype consultation with the professional analyst who is thoroughly familiar with every page of your script and who has worked so hard to give you the guidance to bring your screenplay up to the level where you *should* send it out to agents, producers, and development executives.

In other words…

<u>Don't waste your time sending material around Hollywood without first getting professional review and analysis.</u>

*Screenplays are not works of art.
They are invitations to others to
collaborate on a work of art*

~ Paul Schrader

Afterword

I thought twice about writing this book.

I'm a screenwriter with more than 200 produced film and TV credits. Writing this book is taking me away from my daily work of structuring stories, composing scenes, and writing dialogue. That's the work that feeds the cat, the dog, and everyone else in my family. It's work that I love.

After all, what other professional endeavor allows you to reach out and connect with millions of people around the world through the most compelling visual medium ever devised? There is nothing more impactful than sitting in a darkened movie theatre and watching a film that touches you, moves you, frightens you, or inspires the deepest of human emotions...except being the person who wrote the script eliciting those emotions.

Putting words on paper that express your thoughts and feelings and that are then translated into sound and images in what is arguably our culture's most sophisticated and demanding art form and that then *reach the hearts and minds of an audience* is a magical experience.

That said, it becomes quite a bit less magical when someone discovers what I do for a living and promptly blurts out "I have a great idea for a movie. Let me tell it to you and you can write it and we'll share the credit."

Trust me, I have heard those words on a weekly basis ever since I sold my first script. When I hear them, I usually sigh heavily, take a deep breath, and explain that what I do is my *job* and that "jobs" are how people feed their cat (see above) and I couldn't begin to write someone else's "great idea" without a paycheck attached.

Those who aren't sensitive to economic realities or to the work I've put in to earn my hard-won professional stature then reveal their fragile connection with reality by asking "Okay, when I write it, will you read it and tell me what you think?"

Eye roll. Slow head nod. "Sure. Happy to."

I quickly had a reputation as someone "happy" to read anyone's script and found myself with a stack of scripts sitting on *my* desk sent to me by people whose name I didn't recognize. Long-lost relatives sent me scripts. Former classmates sent me scripts. Perfect strangers with only a passing familiarity with the English language sent me scripts.

Without exception, every single one of those scripts I read as "a favor" fell short of professional caliber. I often wrote lengthy "notes" by way of giving these aspiring writers some meaningful guidance should they persist in the challenges of a screenwriting life. My notes and comments were always positive, sincere, and (silly me) honest. I learned something throughout all of this, an eternal verity: *Nobody wants to hear the truth* when they aren't paying for it.

You may have surmised by now that I have a fairly candid nature. My tendency to speak the truth did not often endear me to those who were hoping my reaction to their screenwriting efforts would be laudatory and include an introduction to a major producer or film star with the clout to get a movie made from their script. I guess my comments like "You really should learn the difference between a pronoun and an artichoke" might have pissed some people off.

Sorry about that.

Then, by way of exploring this growing phenomenon of please-read-my-script-and-tell-me-what-you-think, I dusted off an old low budget screenplay I'd written very early in my career. It had been repeatedly optioned by "producers" who went on to fine careers in the used car business. That particular script, over which I'd sat hunched for a thousand or more hours endlessly rewriting, had consistently won me a series of plum writing assignments whenever I submitted it as a writing sample.

I looked around and saw that the world of spec (non-commissioned) scripts had morphed into an ever-expanding universe of "screenplay contests."

For fifty bucks, I could enter my dusty old horror screenplay into competitions being held from one end of this great country to the other. The East Omaha Screenplay Festival. The Outer Bahamas Script Contest. The 47th Street Hoboken Film & Television Writing Awards. Dozens of others that hardly seemed relevant to the world of professional movie-making.

I dug deeper, looking for a screenplay competition that had at least *some* connection to the actual film and television industry (Omaha's a nice city, but...*come on*). I found a few that appeared to be highly regarded: The Academy Nicholl

Fellowship. The PAGE Screenwriting Awards. Bluecat Screenplay Competition. Slamdance.

I paid my money, entered my low budget screenplay into a handful of the contests.

Ninety to 180 days later, when the winners of these contests were announced, I was either hailed as a brilliant talent by some contests or rebuked as an illiterate clod by others.

Same script. Wildly divergent responses from "industry readers" judging the material.

Hmmm. I wondered what the disconnect could be.

It was at that point that I became curious: who, exactly, are these "readers" passing judgment and ranking the work submitted by legions of screenwriters hoping to find a foothold in Hollywood?

A probing and exhaustive exploration into the ranks of these competition "readers" revealed the scandalous truth: the vast majority of those serving as screenplay contest readers and judges posturing themselves as experts ("Joe Blow has a decade-long history as a development executive at Genius Productions") have never written, produced, or directed anything.

They're not members of any of the industry's professional unions (Writers Guild of America, Directors Guild of America, Screen Actors Guild, Producers Guild of America), and many have never had a *paying* job in the industry (working as an unpaid intern doesn't really carry much weight with me; if you're any good at *anything*, you're getting paid for it).

So who *are* these people judging the vast majority of screenplay competitions?

They are *readers*. Not writers. *Readers*.

Many of these ambitious, well-meaning folks are the product of the nation's recent proliferation of "film schools" popping up like toadstools after a heavy rain. Everybody wants to work in the movies, it seems. (Maybe because making movies looks a lot easier than performing open heart surgery. It's not.)

Colleges and universities from coast-to-coast have discovered a gold mine in students willing to pay astronomical tuition fees in pursuit of their show business dreams.

Graduates of these "film schools" are running around flapping their $100,000 degrees in the wind expecting to become studio development execs or producers just as soon as they get off the bus in Hollywood.

Ain't gonna happen, folks. The reality is that there are no jobs and no assurances of a career path awaiting graduates of these "film studies" programs which have no traditional or direct connection to the professional world of film or television.

Among the courses available at these schools are offerings like "Elements of Mythically Structured Screenwriting" and "Screenplay Principles". Okay, well and good. Tomes like Robert McKee's impenetrable "Story" and Lajos Egri's "The Art of Dramatic Writing" are now the touchstones for students who will likely never sit down to write "Fade In" themselves.

Because those students have no marketable skills to offer an established, unionized industry, the first jobs they're likely to be offered are those as unpaid "interns" or as minimum-wage "readers".

With rare exception, these are the people working as judges at the majority of today's screenplay competitions. These are the people reading your script and giving opinions about your talent. Imagine my personal disappointment to learn that my low budget screenplay (again, repeatedly optioned) only came in second place in the eyes of these completely inexperienced industry analysts!

So I made a decision.

I decided it was time to provide a screenwriting competition where *the judging means something because the judges are all proven industry professionals.*

I recruited more than a dozen Hollywood professionals; people with more than a century of collective industry experience. Directors. Screenwriters. Producers. Agents. Actors. Filmmakers. Each and every one of them has a powerful resume and an impressive credit history based upon projects that have actually been *produced* and seen by millions of people.

These are all members of the Hollywood guilds who have the training and decades of solid industry working experience seeing screenplays turned into world-class movies and TV shows.

These would be the best screenwriting judges on the planet. The result: The Los Angeles International Screenplay Awards (www.lascreenplayawards.com) is now among the most highly respected script competitions you can find. It's the place where judging is in the hands of people who know what the craft truly demands and what today's market is looking for.

I'm not a "born writer" by any stretch of the imagination. I began exactly where you are today, with zero industry contacts and only a vague idea of what writers do. It didn't happen overnight, but someone took the time to give me some guidance, and eventually I began to sell my writing and wound up with a career I could never have dreamed of.

If it happened to me, I know it can happen to you!

I sincerely hope everything I've said here encourages you to keep writing and to get your screenplay into the kind of professional shape that propels it into the winner's circle and then onto movie screens around the world.

I love hearing from my readers, so feel free to send comments and questions (no scripts, please!) via email to me at bbmscripts@gmail.com. I promise to do my best to respond personally to you.

Until then, remember the most important key to winning any screenplay competition: Keep writing and enter the best contests you can find!

How to *WIN* Your Next Screenplay Contest

*Screenwriting is like ironing.
You move forward a little bit and
go back and smooth things out.*

~ Paul Thomas Anderson, screenwriter

Frequently Asked Questions

I've learned that even after people understand all of the preceding and have a firm grasp on *how to win their next screenplay contest*, they still have a few questions rattling around in the back of their minds.

I completely understand. Screenwriting contests are tough to navigate and it's hard to know if you're entering the right ones. I hope the following will shed some light on those issues.

Q: *There are so many contests to choose from. How do I know which ones are any good?*

A: Look at two things:
1. Who are the judges reviewing submitted scripts? Are they experienced film and television professionals...or just a bunch of unnamed "readers"? You don't want

to get involved with amateurs at any level.
2. Where are the contests located? If they aren't in Hollywood or New York, or a major center of the arts (Austin, for example) , take a pass.

Q: *How long does it take to get my script read, reviewed, and judged?*

A: The best competitions will take a minimum of 30 days to review materials submitted by their deadline. That's because good judges and reviewers read every single word of your script. If you can enter on the deadline date and winners are announced within less than 30 days, scripts aren't being properly evaluated.

Q: *How long should a good contest last?*

A: A minimum of 90 days. Anything less, and the contest operators are just trying to churn submissions as quickly as they can without providing proper reading and analysis in their judging process.

Q: *How many judges does a good contest have?*

A: The number of judges isn't nearly as important as their professional backgrounds, so avoid any contest that doesn't name each and every judge. Fewer than a half-dozen named judges would be a red flag.

Q: *If I win a contest, will they produce my script?*

A: No. Judging good material and getting it produced are two different things. But a good contest will help the winners get their scripts into the marketplace where the best producers are on the lookout for the best scripts.

Q: *Can I enter the same script in more than one contest at a time?*

A: Yes. And you should. Winning or placing well in more than one recognized competition will give your script the opportunity for greater industry exposure.

Q: *When I win a contest, what should I do next?*

A: Immediately post it on all your social media profiles, send out emails to everyone in your contact list, and shout it from the rooftops. Winning a contest is a big deal, but it's up to you to tell the world about it.

Q: *How do I know someone at the screenplay contest won't rip off my idea or sell my script with their name on it?*

A: Legitimate screenplay competitions are run by industry professionals who know that once you've written something, <u>you own the copyright outright</u>. People who plagiarize or violate copyright laws face a variety of potentially serious legal penalties. Guaranteeing your protected rights in your material is easy: just put your name on your script, register it with the Writers Guild of America, only enter reputable contest like the The Los Angeles International Screenplay Awards (http://www.lascreenplayawards.com), and you'll have nothing to worry about.

The key is—don't monkey around with the script. Then everything usually goes pretty well.

~ Steven Soderbergh, director

About the Author

Robert L. McCullough has more than 200 produced credits in film and television.

Bob and his wife Suzanne live in Santa Barbara and co-host host the celebrity podcast series *Where Hollywood Hides*. Their book *Where Hollywood Hides: Celebrities in Paradise* is a popular seller at Amazon.com.

Bob holds degrees from U.S.C., the University of Texas, The American Film Institute, and Southwestern University School of Law. An Emeritus member of Writers Guild of America, his complete credit history is available at www.IMDB.com.

Now that you've read this book...

Shouldn't you be writing?

Made in the USA
Las Vegas, NV
27 August 2023

76711139R00069